AF266804

You're Only Crazy If You Answer

B. Sonenreich

merigold independent
www.merigoldindependent.com
Atlanta, GA

Sonenreich, B.

Edited by Olamma Oparah
Cover design by Jordan B. Kady

Printed in the United States of America

IBSN: 9781088082508

MERIGOLD INDEPENDENT

For Foti

"your slightest look easily will unclose me"

E.E. Cummings

Contents

You're Only Crazy If You Answer — 1
The Successive Lover — 2
404 Error Code — 5
The Vanishing of 1/3 of 3 Lovers — 6
What do I do with all of this love? — 7
memory is a ruptured space — 8
Annunciation of a Newcomer — 9
food for flowers — 11
a word within a word — 12
closure at the local café — 13
A Prerequisite to Knowing — 14
An Education — 16
A Pardoning — 17
looking through the wrong end of a kaleidoscope — 18
Electroencephalogram — 19
agoraphobia vs. autophobia — 20
the ball drops [as does the other shoe] — 21
long ago, it must be — 22
my mother said she liked you — 23
[appliance] care on memorial drive — 25
when the light went out — 27
i am still here — 28
Φώτης — 29

You're Only Crazy If You Answer

They say
you're only
crazy if you answer,

yourself
as you pace
the tar stained
sidewalks
talking to no one,
and everyone
at the same time.

The Successive Lover

Formerly known as "rebound,"
the successive lover serves
their function

And the sex is like
having the last bite
of dessert,
knowing well
you're already full

The stove
still partially lit
a mess of a sink
half clean
plates towering

The backsplash
tiled red, like the
crevices of your mind

Agh; you,
squeamish,
excuse yourself
to a
wallpapered bathroom
after you're done
with the successive
love making
and you look
long in the mirror

You convince yourself
not to puke in the nearby pot.

"Come back to bed,"
the successive lover
might call out

Still draped
in your sheets,
more a suggestion
than a demand

Even the term
successive
sounds like
a ball
swishing
through a net

It's worse than
a rebound
It's having
a connection
go through you
seamlessly

It escaped me

Successive

Not first,
not last,
but an
in between
space
where
the warmth
is only
a comforting
disguise

and
all the while,
my house is on fire

your constant lack of response says something along the lines of the server cannot find the requested resource which feels almost like flirting

The Vanishing of 1/3 of 3 Lovers

A looping sensation
of perpetually backing out
of lovers' drives
Perhaps a lifelong sentence
of reverse motion
I continue to sit
comfortably uncomfortable
waiting for anyone to stop me
But as I arrive back home,
uncalled for but
not necessarily unmissed,
I flip directly to Bukowski's "3 Lovers"
An urge to channel
the writer's drunken rage,
only to realize that

I only have animosity
for leaving itself;

the visceral nature of it all,
it's ability to shapeshift
between interactions only
to be stripped down,
waving its hands, guiltily
revealing the identical purpose
of the last.

A feeling of constantly driving
but never reaching a destination.
Yet, I continue
to leave them there
to do
whatever
they wanted to
do.

What do I do with all of this love?

Do I beg you to take it from me? Do I plead for you to stay while I unpack it and set it into piles to reallocate amongst friends and family? Do I sleep with it? Where should I place it? Between my legs with other sacred things? Perhaps under my pillow (so I can take it out and look at it when I should be asleep). Are you certain you don't want it? Or is it at the very least uncertainly unwanted? Do you think about where I've stored it? Have you wondered if I'll repurpose it for someone else? Maybe something: a comforting feline, a ferocious dog, a grand piano, a classic guitar? Did you ever imagine me shoving it into a sterile space? A storage unit overflowing with my love for you. Something with a passcode and a monthly fee to keep it safe, but at a distance. Can we imagine my love — this gushy, sticky substance, warm and inviting yet all encompassing — in a box? It can be a handmade wooden vessel with carvings that tell our unique story. I take comfort in knowing my love for you would be in an artifact. I'd keep it safe with my crystal teacups and family heirlooms. We wouldn't have to concern ourselves with where to store all of my love for you. Untarnished, without tangle. It will stay safe and snug. But most of all, it will stay.

memory is a ruptured space

Veiled in precarious alibis
Versions of unspoken truth
Too cowardly
Two faced

Memory is
a ruptured space

I actively forget
Your acts of kindness
Immersed in the heat
A Wednesday in July

Found myself in
Old haunts
Wrapping my limbs
around a dead dream
You spoke
to everyone,
but me

A strategy to survive
the loss of you

A mistake,
or an orchestrated incident
When you asked yourself
Do you really
like being alone?

of course you don't

Annunciation of a Newcomer

A pyromaniac
enticed with a porcelain ashtray
overflowing free matchbooks

A mixture of offerings
drugs and booze
at a fixed price
of zero

The first time in thirty years
strapped to the proverbial wagon

It can't be easy,
she said to me,
with admiration
for the person
I'm becoming

Easy
was walking away
from everything
that meant something
for a hit,
for a swig

The menacing reflection
in the looking glass
has never been so simple
to stare back at

Beginning to trust myself

I dig a hole in black sand
submerge my head
and breathe earth

What's hard[ening]
are the white caps of realization
coming at me
full force

How easy it was walking away from you
who meant everything
for a hit,
for a swig

food for flowers

When near death
Peonies look their most vivacious
Stems bunched up in tap water
Longing for roots
Were we the same?
Could I predict
The impending expiration date
Through the bursting of petals?
He loves me not

a word within a word

You have survived
in the elastic flaps
of my mind

Crystalized in the why,
I am so full
of shit

In the same instance
brimming
with hope

Flagrant lies
weaved into
tearful testimonies

Permeable to
air
oil
grease
bacteria
water

Made of cellophane
These truths,
turned stories

Amends sans mend
As they should outlast
The both of us

closure at the local café

we process our loss
over lukewarm cups of coffee
scars that won't fade
eavesdropping strangers
heard voices cracking
a poorly paved sidewalk
alongside the congested street
canopied with trees
older than both of us
i used to skip to field trips
macaws and parakeets
too loud to internalize silence
often the only gift
i receive
after 365 days of lying
wind chills are still
foreign territory
the holidays full of
historic feelings
clenched jaws
wishing fondness
in the chosen vocabulary
anyone would use for me

A Prerequisite to Knowing

I applied myself in courses
None of which lectured or assigned
The lessons a student must learn
To ultimately survive
Forgiveness can contain loss
As loss can breathe forgiveness
Moments of happiness tinged with despair
And despair in times of happiness
Present tensions when sifting through pastimes
Covert answers in our formulaic responses

That not all that age die
Fermenting truths surfacing new whys
And, perhaps by surprise, we pry
Open one another
Only to recognize shards
Of mirrors beneath rows of cracked ribs
How seamless attachments
Are made in unexpected connections
And then, just as easily,
Bulldozed as a result of a billion fracture points
Those moments of minuscule reprieve
I remember
A crimson door
And the conversations behind it
But instead, I tend to dwell on the silence
Simmering like a finely greased pan
Above a spontaneously lit pilot light
I know there's no longer an entryway
Into love gone awry
But to alleviate sleepless nights
I go on haunting the doorframe of dialectics
And you might not notice

But on the off chance that you do,
I hope you don't mind

An Education

Teach me how to love
By leaving me
In the blurred space
Between knowing
And unknowing you
A blunt curriculum in deprivation:
The essence of a gradual death
So calm and yet still unaware
Of what to expect
A syllabus of steady contemplation -
Where I've traced over memories
Like dimples so deep
I could sink into them

A Pardoning

I once reprimanded
your lack of manners
Now I say *thank you*
for cutting me off
Bursts of catharsis
Amidst months of yearning
When I began to use you
Like all of my other vices
Like you were a means to an end
Like a cheap salve retrieved from
a medicine cabinet
Now it's my turn to say
Please, forgive me for not knowing
how to be cared for

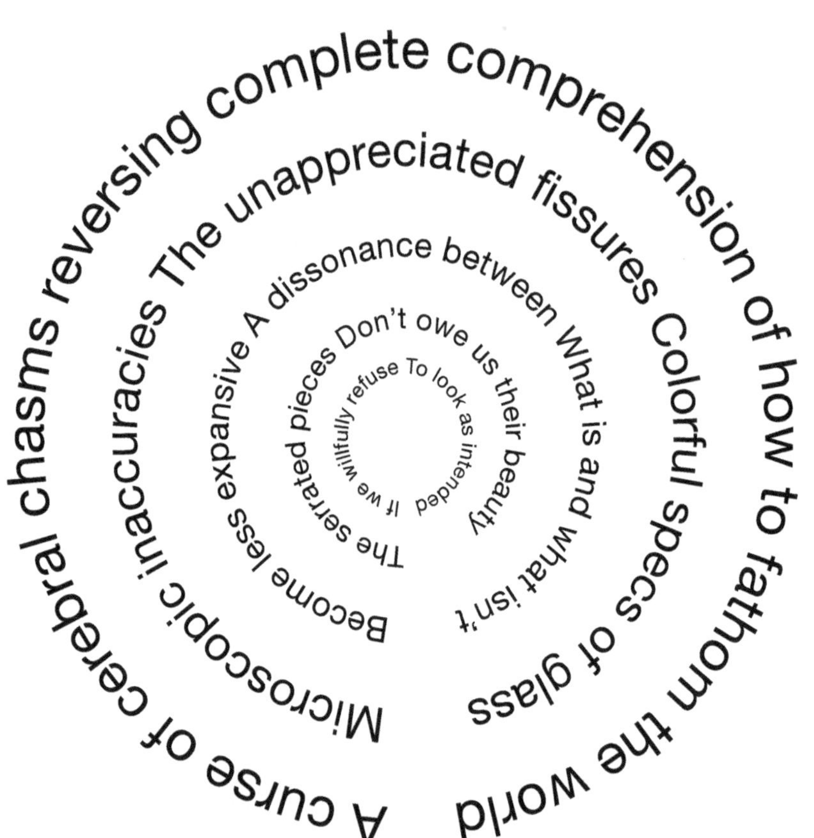
A curse of cerebral chasms reversing complete comprehension of how to fathom the world
Microscopic inaccuracies The unappreciated fissures Colorful specs of glass
Become less expansive A dissonance between What is and what isn't
The serrated pieces Don't owe us their beauty
If we willfully refuse To look as intended

Electroencephalogram

Each moment
Encapsulates a certain loveliness
Especially the instances of adulation
Even the ones of pain
Ever changing ideas of how to approach a lover
Expectations differ, the only constant: change
Endless gratitude and the
Epitome of remorse
Episodic love affair, a fear of
Ending in divorce

agoraphobia vs. autophobia

Your lack of speech
Was mistook
For my being ignored

Commence the fear of
Me packing up my coats
My scarves
My trinkets
The bottle of shampoo
The conditioner and soaps
The spare toothbrush
From the vanity you called mine
The spices and oils
From the kitchen cabinets
The half burnt sage
From the dusty window sill
The papier-mâché trophy
Spray painted gold
An underlying fear
That I'd stop thinking of you
As beloved
Or worse,
That I'd stop thinking of you
At all

While all you were doing
Was praying for me
To be okay
Alone

the ball drops [as does the other shoe]

Our passion was a delectable fire
Similar to the one I stand in front of
This New Year's Eve
In the backyard of a married friend's home
She invited me to this weeks prior
But I am sober now
She insisted
There were more of my kind in attendance
I no longer receive your kisses at midnight
And I drive home alone
Counting my blessings at every red light
Shyly hoping not to hit a pothole
Lest I have more time to ponder
Both past and future selves
And how they both miss you

long ago, it must be

Memory, sealed
Into the moulding
Of a home renovated
A stairway creaking
beneath
The encapsulation
Imagine bare wood
My toes pondering
the edge of each step
I do fear heights
as I fear love
Translucent little things
That raise my heartbeat
That raise my expectations
Pulsing passion in a
particular predicament
Before it got complicated
What was it prior
to this moment?
Plummeting beneath
Here in the basement
Where you keep your bikes
and your tools
Where I'd sometimes bring
down your laundry
Or dance without reserve
"Bookends" on repeat
We've mastered brevity
and bonds that don't keep

my mother said she liked you

You were honest

No promises
of permanence
or a white picket fence
holding caramel children
in the yard

Tapered expectations

You never let me run
too far
with my own
imagination

Although,
my original notion:
only one way
to get sober

Nine months
of growing
a being as large
as a bowling ball

Several years
of small hands
and feet
crawling onto
surfaces
Our kitchen table
Our cabinets
Our king sized bed
Ourselves

Pregnant with nothing
and sober nonetheless
I dress myself every day

A recognition
of addiction
is a thin line
on an alleyway

Deciphering the area
I could
slip and fall

New predicaments
faced dry
A fleeting dream,
but nothing more

No reservations
for four

[appliance] care on memorial drive

There's a man fixing
Appliances next door
A black and mild
Hanging from his mouth
He doesn't smell
Of you

I type,
The small details
Envelope
Large moments

What you smell like
To her

Does she bury her face
Into your armpits
To breathe in
Solace
Like I did

I've been sleeping alone
For ~~days~~, ~~weeks~~, months

Never short
Of profanities

Slipping in
And out of
A cement studio

Where I used to bring
Coffee over ice
With a shot of
Chocolate;

How you used to like it

Or have you cut
It out
Like my presence

Choices you make
To stay healthy

The man next door,
Intent on repairing pasts
Carried out
By strangers

I'm afraid,
Dedicating this
To you
Will fix
Nothing.

when the light went out

I am convinced
Hellbent
On minor assurances
The poor timing
Of lights metering traffic
You lingering at an exit
Huffing into your gut
Me withholding commands
Wondering if there's a U-turn
Where we can go back to that Monday
And eat our words
I'll oversimplify
And say, *I still care*
We will take advantage of the silence
Obsessing over waking up to you
The only thing that exceeds
Sleeping together

i am still here

succumbing to the circumference
of my arms wrapped around your belly
do you too
reminisce
talking at length
our lore
the abuse we inflicted
on half-innocent souls
in public places
and under covers
or the taste of strawberries
dipped in granulated sugar
how both our fathers
preferred hospitals
over family dinners
and how no matter how many
people call us geniuses
we still cannot tell
the difference
between cumulus and stratus
clouding our judgment
the conversations we had
about everything
about nothing

Φώτης

celestial fondness

my planet

orbiting your light

casting the same pattern

an ouroboros makes

in Greek antiquity

swallowing my own tail

in an alternate universe

where we have

over a trillion years

to process the start

to prepare for

the end

Acknowledgments

I am deeply grateful for my editor and confidante, Olamma Oparah. Olamma is poetic in her very essence, and raises Anyanwu with unmatched grace. His shine is from you.

Thank you to Samuel Laubscher and merigold independent, who believed in this book before I was able to wrap my mind around finishing it. Additional thanks to Jordan B. Kady, who designed the cover with her whole heart.

An innumerable amount of thank yous go out to my sister, Katrina; for always being there, for radiance in the darkest of times, and for constantly asking questions — even ones I still don't know how to answer.

And to you, my reader: thank you. I hope you always find relief in loss, or someone who, at the very least, will listen.

B. Sonenreich is a writer and film theorist. She graduated with her BA in creative writing from Florida State University and her MA in communication from Georgia State University.

When she's not watching movies or listening to music, she's taking her dog Keaton for 4 walks a day in Atlanta, Georgia.

www.ingramcontent.com/pod-product-compliance
Lightning Source LLC
Chambersburg PA
CBHW050046040726

47599CB00015B/1827